THE
GRUMPY OLD
WELSHMAN

3rd (and last) EDITION

A
GRUMPY OLD
WELSHMAN

by
LEWAS-AP-FOOTE

1st Edition 10.6.2004
2nd Edition 01.3.2006

Published 2012

Publisher Gareth G. Woodham

© Lewas-ap-Foote

ISBN 978-0-9574854-0-2

With Love To
Ann Jane

AUTHOR'S NOTE

Where poems in this book refer to public officials that are no longer in office – or institutions that have now been done away with – they were written before the event.

Introduction

This little book, now in its Third Edition and Hardback, is, I hope, the crystallisation (and final) shot after a long and costly battle with local, regional and national bureaucracy. I have retired and become super-animated!

If I had not written the book "The Grumpy Old Welshman", it is likely that, like so many disgruntled businessmen, entrepreneurs and local mavericks, I would have landed up in prison.

This book has allowed me to put my point of view, something denied to 'middle Wales' man. The media in Wales sells itself on a thread of Welsh celebrity, sporting personality or myth. A shallow purchase. No criticism of the powerful people, boring and a danger to advertising. The vendettas in Carmarthen, the pier up North, the hippies in Powys etc. etc.

I estimate that in the last ten years, the twenty two unitary authorities in Wales have spent well in excess of £70million pounds of ratepayers money on wasted legal and planning battles against people like myself. Set against this, the Welsh Planning Application Appeals etc. Land being abandoned. This land has value and will win through in some agreed form. Therefore, you ask, what a waste of resource, of peoples time and councils' budgets. Petty local politics (read Bernard Levin, page)

The saddest part of it all is that in the Welsh Ashambly, hailed as "democracy in Wales" are aware of the local authority abuses but have done nothing about it. To do so would require taking over and controlling the little man in the Council (ref. again Bernard Levin). Dear Old Ron Davies had done the mollified deal – support the Welsh Assembly. Carry on your spite.

Prior to the launching of the Second Edition on St. David's Day, March 1 2006, my publisher thought that rather than grumbling at the state, large and small, I should do something positive to coincide with the second issue.

I chose a subject in the poems "The Severn Lake" (page 79) and after studying the history of the Severn Barrage Scheme, found that no-one had ever deposited a planning application, and yet there were fourteen thousand documents on the subject alone, on the internet.

I cobbled together my own plan and super crazy 'visionary' scheme, filled in the forms and spent approximately £250 per shore i.e. Vale of Glamorgan and Somerset Councils' with a "Change of Use" planning application to change the Severn River to the Severn Lake. This was 145,000 hectares of water that could produce 7% of the nations electricity power. The rest is history, and my part will come out in a book yet to be written – The Severn Lake (Pre the Predators)

Sadly, my prediction in my Introduction of the Second Edition published 01/03/06 was to forecast the demise of our economy in 2007. I now await my fifth boom, predicted to peak (with apologies) in 2016.

Finally, before you smile on and hopefully agree with the moanings, grumblings, rantings, of enhancing our lives in this land of opportunity, predictions, past and present, and my efforts to bring real prosperity to Wales, let me yet again lead you to wonder (page 48) 'Why do we Spite our Own'. What is it about the people that the Welsh put into power, and the people in local government, there to serve us, that make them resent and punish and spite us so disgracefully instead of enhancing our lives in this wonderful land, Wales.

01.03.2012

Introduction

(from the first book of 10.6.2004)

This little book of poems and bits arose from an article in The Times by Bernard Levin (1991). My own frustration at my local Council, it seems, was similar to that felt by millions of people. In 1987 I returned from Austria, where you were unlikely to see a toffee paper on the street, whilst at home, I struggled ankle deep in litter to collect my post alongside the main railway station at Neath. Could I vent my anger to just a few local people to get the town cleaned up? Posters were circulated.

My next foray was a letter to The Times.

The country was being sold off; railways, Rolls Royce (to Volkswagon), Rover (to BMW). You name it, some other country was buying UK Plc. They would not publish my letter. Damned annoying!

I was a little busy in the early nineties. Booming and busting, we self employed call it. Remember 15% interest (base) rates and paying 20% on an overdraft!

Then around '92ish it got very quiet, so I found time to write a little more and found it a pressure relief valve, just to write it down.

Family and friends found my new engagement handy, poems for weddings, birthdays, successes etc. until it was suggested (I cannot for the moment pin the blame on anyone specifically), that I should gather together all my little rantings and, yes, you are reading them.

Of all my poems, the one that will stick out as a real mystic was the one called "Devolution". I sat on Mr. Vincent Kane's car at the Trinity College Carmarthen, the night before the vote and we both agreed that no way would the people of Wales vote for the Devolution. (I certainly did not know that it would not require a majority of Welsh people, but a quarter, as it turned out). Little did we know how the real events would mirror the prophecy in the poem.

I have kept things simple, mean no harm and hope to do a little good.

Remember, it has cost me as much as you, for you to be able to read this book.

Please enjoy.

Lewas-ap-Foote.

Introduction

(from the second book of 1.3.2006)

For many years, I have been writing poetry inspired by my anger over a number of local issues that have been affecting – crippling, in fact – Welsh businesses and the Welsh economy. I began putting my poems and bits and pieces of writing together – and in July 2004 published the first edition of A Grumpy Old Welshman.

Less than a month later, I was saddened to hear that Bernard Levin, whose article "Councils of Despair" I had included in my first edition, had passed away. I realised that it would be necessary to bring out an update of the book as soon as I could manage it.

But two other things also prompted me to begin work on a second edition.

Firstly, I overheard Mrs Gwenda Thomas, Ashambly Member for Neath, speaking to her loyal husband. What I heard was her saying that she hoped she had not made an appearance in my book, and especially that I had not criticised her. She said that to be included seemed to have been the 'kiss of death' to several careers. The day before she'd read my book, which severely criticised the Welsh Development Agency, the government announced that the agency was to be dissolved. After I heard her comments, I went back to my book, and I realised she was right; they were all gone: Clapham Ron, Alan Michael, Goodway, Jones, Crawley, the WDA – and Lord Hain soon to be put out to grass. It was obvious I needed to bring the book up to date.

Secondly, I hope to help businesses survive 2007. I will try to promote and push 'George's Law' (see Contents Page), because, without this scheme, or one like it, employing staff will eventually cease for small business. To conclude, I would like to say that I also have a selfish reason for bringing out a second edition. People's reaction to the first edition has given me huge satisfaction. It really seems to have made people laugh. Many Welsh wives have confirmed to me that the Grumpy Old Welshman lives with them. There is even talk of a Grumpy Old Welshman's club. I bet no-one will find a hall big enough to hold them all!

Enjoy.

Lewas ap Foote

Contents

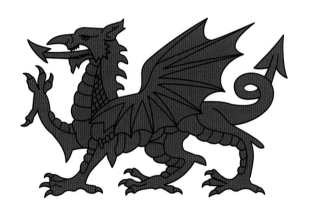

Middle Wales – Saviours in Limbo

The working class, in Wales only vote for their own, therefore you get working class labour every time (hence the donkey-tail joke)

Historically, (the last one hundred years), Wales has been ruled by the working class Labour MP's (or AM) but these MP's now with huge power have become the elite, celebrities, wealthy (the Kinnocks – George Thomas, James Callaghan, Rhodri Morgan etc). Their problem, however, is so……

The inward looking working class know nothing of the world of business, or the economy. So they look to their MP's (AM's) to run the economy of Wales. It is unfortunate that the indigenous Welsh Business is not supported by working class MP's or AM's, because they are old Labour, and private business make that socialist evil 'a profit'. (Ironically, this does not apply to Korean, Japanese or American Investors). The working class and their MP's have not yet worked out that the profits made in Wales by foreign companies return home to their countries.

So here we have middle Wales. Held up in the planning system, unable to get hold of Welsh money grants, starved of finance being sidelined by money given to local authority grand schemes (objective one, wasted opportunity).

Now, the conundrum. The Labour elite need to grow Wales. Their one hundred years have failed, but they need middle Wales. But how to court middle Wales without betraying their party or constituents.

They, through their politics, their position and, now, their wealth, have moved in the World, out of Wales. The old enemy, England, does better than Wales, then there is Europe? The answer is clear, but how the method, how not to betray the Welsh working class?

This, I suggest, is why the Welsh Assembly Government was set up with 40 constituency AM's and 20 regional AM's. 40 Welsh working class, and 20 of the chosen ones with no working class allegiance. It has not worked yet. This is because, like all corrupt regimes, there has to be truth and reconciliation. I put to you that all the MP's and AM's over the last fifty years are aware of the spite that has been meted out to middle Wales by the Rulers in Wales over the last one hundred years. But they are: (a) in denial, and (b) unwilling to deal, in any way, with the perpetrators, Local and Regional Labour Controlled Councils.

So, it is my opinion that the hard working class of Wales, by their own actions, keep Wales the poor working class nation of the United Kingdom.

The indigenous Welsh Businesses are <u>middle Wales</u>, they are also employers, entrepreneurs, innovators, (replacing the mine owners in the 'Big House' on the hill). But will they ever rise up and face up to the old working class labour and demand an honest opportunity to create much needed employment to grow Wales – "and make it profitable"?

15th August 2012

Councils of Despair

The Little Man in his Office
Cannot resist wielding his tiny power.

I knew Bernard Levin before I had read his many twice weekly articles for the Times over the twenty-five years or more that he worked there. It struck me, that, as a boy I would always make sure to return home on a Saturday evening, where a warm iced sponge cake with cherries on top would be waiting, and David Frost (now Sir), Lance Percival, Millicent Martin and a sketch by Bernard Levin (and a studio audience) would be on the telly. (He was twice assaulted). A whole slab of sponge cake could disappear during that programme!

Levin wrote of mendacious statesmen, nasty regimes, faceless bureaucrats, asinine jobsworths and grasping lawyers, all of whom had messed up the lives of ordinary people. At the Times, in some two thousand articles, he wrote on everything from the failings of the public utilities, banks, railways, airlines and the oppression of minorities. He wrote for the underdog and against the bullies. In his writings, for forty years, he made the powerful furious and the powerless grateful. I was one of the latter.

Bernard Levin died after many years of illness on 7 August 2004. He was a stimulus for "A Grumpy Old Welshman" and I too want to make the powerful furious and the powerless grateful.

Read on. 11.08.04
Author's note

The Times, London 3 October 1991

Councils of Despair

*The Little Man in his office cannot
resist wielding his tiny power.*

When I see a headline reading "Man takes law into his own hands to bury bungalow" I prick up my ears. I have seen all sorts of sights in my long life, including a totally plastered Cabinet minister falling down two flights of stairs and I simply cannot understand how he was doing it. (The bungalow man, not the Cabinet minister).

So I examined the subject more closely, and when I had fully understood how (to say nothing of why) a man would bury his bungalow, I was rather less amused. Indeed, I made haste to wipe the smile off my face. For this story is far from funny.

Mr. Trevor Sedgbeer and his wife Lauretta live in Devon, and Mr. Sedgbeer built a bungalow; many do, and in this case did. But he built his bungalow – italic, printers, for the awfulness of what now comes: he built his bungalow without planning permission. Now, short of murder, there is nothing so wicked as a man who builds a bungalow without planning permission, or, to be more exact, there is nothing so wicked as a man who builds his bungalow when the man who deals out permissions has not given his say-so.

I have said a thousand times that power should be used upside down; the bigger the slice of it the more wary the user should be, and vice versa. And when it comes to a Devon bungalow permission-giver, the very tiniest scrap of the heady stuff should be used only with the head immersed in a bowl of very cold water.

It is not clear whether the offence was that the bungalow was in the wrong place, or whether it had not been approved, or both. But after much wrangling, the course demanded the destruction of Mr. Sedgbeer's bungalow.

Mr. Sedgbeer complied with the order to destroy the bungalow, which came down flat. Now I have, in my time, done some rum things, but never before have I found myself invited to go about digging holes for bungalows, and politely demurred. But on inquiring further, I learnt that to bury a bungalow means shifting several hundred tons of earth. It seems that Mr. Sedgbeer was in earnest when he said that he would give the authorities their wish with knobs on – several hundred tons of knobs. The battle continued;

18

for a time, any member of the council passing by would have seen nothing but the flatness that had been required. But then, it seems, that at least as the council would have it, Mr. Sedgbeer's home had risen from the earth – grimy no doubt – and the struggle was renewed: was the earth flat enough, or had Mr. Sedgbeer merely repeated his crime/ He says: "I have obeyed the court ruling by taking the building down to the original ground level of the site. I have done all they have asked me to do." It is not for me to adjudicate, but what chills my blood is those terrible, those most terrible words, which came from the lips of someone in the council (they always come from the lips of someone in the council): "We cannot allow one person to contravene the law while making others abide by it. We are determined that the building should be removed."

Oh, sing it to the birds, play it on the accordion, whistle it while you work but it will still be the same ancient rubic: "What if everybody did it?"

What indeed – for Mr. Sedgbeer has just been put in prison for a three month stretch for not destroying his home at the council's behest.

Oh, what if everybody did it? I am tempted to answer that the council members would be beside themselves with joy.

But now we must go from Devon to Leicestershire. Here, there is no tinge of amusement, even if there was before. A Mr. Pickavant had an 18th century cottage on his farmland, which he was lovingly restoring. But the council (oh, yes, there is always someone from the council) said to Mr. Pickavant that there could be only one dwelling on the farm, a bungalow, which Pickavant senior would occupy. But the 18th century dwelling was for Pickavant junior, who was to live in it with his lady. But if there is a bungalow and an 18th century cottage on the same farm – well, two ones make two.

Mr. Sedgbeer was reasonably young and sprightly. Mr. Pickavant is 67, and when his struggle began (oh, yes, there was a struggle) he collapsed; he came round just in time to see his world crushed. And crushed is the right word, because the council (oh, yes, yes, yes, there was someone from the council to watch, and for all I know to look smug) had engaged ten policemen – six of whom were in riot gear – and a giant digger. And the digger was not a toy one. It worked.

And the work of four years (not counting the people in the 18th century who started the cottage) was destroyed.

Yes, yes, yes, the law is the law and must be obeyed. Mr. Pickavant had already been fined £500, and a judge had said he was "stubborn and foolish", which indeed he probably was, though it would be a good idea if the judge in question took a 40-year holiday.

But that again is not the point. The point is that someone from the council said – oh, but you know what I am going to say now – the people from the council said: "If we failed to enforce the order, it would open the floodgates for everyone else to build houses without planning permission in the countryside."

Ah, the angels weep; you can hear them clearly if the wind is in the right direction. And their tears speak volumes: "enforce the order", "floodgates", "contravene the law", "if we failed to", "while making others abide by it", "planning permission", "planning permission", "planning permission".

But now we are in the countryside, where things are done differently, but if we pack up and head for the smoky air of the town, do not think that councils have disappeared and we can smile. Because Mr. Brian Godfrey of Ilkeston has nothing to smile about.

He is a greengrocer by trade, and he displays his wares on the pavement, as countless greengrocers have done through the ages. Indeed, I am told that that has been at the same site in Ilkeston for some 30 years at least.

Of course, his boxes are put against the window of his shop, not on the kerb side, and of course he pays rent to the council for a foot and a half of the pavement. But Mr. Godfrey has now come up against the same kind of people as those you have just been reading about.

Thirty years have passed with this familiar scene, but now the council (well, of course it was the council – who did you think it was?) has decided to puff out its chest and ruin Mr. Godfrey. It claims that his 18inches of pavement are dangerous, especially for the blind or disabled people, though it seems that there has been no accident at all with Mr. Godfrey's wares. He says:

People like to see fresh fruit and vegetables in front of the shop, not through the window. It is something you see in high streets everywhere. It is ridiculous to suggest I have no heed for safety. I have had no complaints, but the council cannot accept that they might be wrong. We have customers who are in wheelchairs. Except for the council, nobody has complained.

When Mr. Godfrey stood his ground and ignored the council (hurrah!), he was taken to court by Derbyshire County Council – there's splendour for you! – and the wowsers lost! The magistrates – may the sun shine upon them

– ruled that he was not causing an obstruction. The victorious Mr. Godfrey, as a handsome token of reconciliation, announced that he was going to halve the space of his display. And what followed? But you know, of course, what followed.

Smarting from the defeat, the council asked the High Court to overturn the magistrates' ruling. And alas, it did. The judge – may he get chilblains – gave the wrong answer. And you could hear the smug smiles on the faces of the county council. And another innocent, useful, happy, hard-working man is ruined. And oh, yes, you will certainly know what comes now in this case. Yes, the boss man did say – these were the very words: "If we made an exception for Mr. Godfrey, a precedent could have been set which could have affected the rights of pavement users throughout the Country". That's glory for you!

Remember the Rule? The rule that says the smaller the quantity of power the greater the yearning to exercise it? And have I now just demonstrated that sad truth?

The Times London 3rd October 1991

21

Feeling strongly about the issue of Neath's littered streets, I distributed this flier in Neath in 1987

"Keep Neath Dirty Campaign"

To Start

More effort is needed. We are only ankle deep in litter. Let us all make a supreme effort. 'Knee deep by Christmas'. Throw away this sheet. No one will prosecute you. Look around you; everyone is throwing cans, litter, etc.

Employment

More rubbish on the streets means More Jobs. You will be helping the unemployment situation.

Countryside Initiative

Greater emphasis must be placed on the Neath Tourist Areas. We know you've tried, but whilst the town is a real mess, out in the country, you've only just started. 'Think Big'. Never mind about plastic bags, garden refuse, tissues, rubber goods! Come out of an evening, pick up a Kentucky Fried Wimpy (their container colours go well with the grass), a six pack, an old mattress etc. Tip the lot. (Why not empty your ash trays while you're there – there's nothing a sheep likes better than a good choke!)

WARNING
Be aware of litter wardens and rubbish bins – in Neath???

"The Stasi Building"

Letter to the Editor

The Times
1 Pennington Street
LONDON E1 9XN 09.09.94

Dear Sir,

Re: The Right Team for the Job

If the Russian Leaders, in power before 1979, had come up with a plan to bring Britain to its knees, it would have been hard pressed to find a better group to do this job than the present Government.

Yours faithfully,

Lewas ap-Foote

Neath: Dirty Little Town

Ten years since the Australians played the Gnoll
Much money spent on bins and funds to trawl the streets for litter,
Dirty Little Town.

Campaigns have failed to change the dirty little people in this
Dirty Little Town
Filling the streets with litter,
Dirty Little Town.

Grazers from Tesco's and Safeways and more
'Drop' on the corners, the bends, the roundabouts,
Cans and bags and take away litter,
Dirty Little Town.

The trains and the buses deposit their armies
To fast food outlets whose pavements smell of grease and chips and litter,
Dirty Little Town,

Smokers whose lives are led dropping ash and ends, have
Inbuilt skills with the full list of cans and bags, matches,
Sweets papers, 'bedspreads' and litter
Dirty Little Town.

Weekend mornings from the night before
Provide a whole industry of sweepers, brushes, drivers, carts
Waste disposal profits to fat Directors dealing in Litter, Dirty Little Town.

To criticise is easy, answers are easy
One must provide wardens with body armour and automatic
Weapons
To fine the people who drop litter in this,
Dirty Little Town.

But the locals love the town,
They fail to see what others abhor
But the people are changing
The green-field estates will see the litter in this,
Dirty Little Town.

I won't, I'm leaving!

01.09.97

The Welsh Economy

(A) Proposal for 22,000 Jobs

(B) WDA "Thoughts" "Critique"

(C) Article – South Wales Evening Post

(D) Was Alan Michael (Minister for Rural Affairs '03 '04) Listening in 1999?

The Times 05.01.04

(A) Proposal for 22,000 Jobs

The following proposal for 22,000 Jobs in Wales was put to David Roe Beddoe, Chairman of the WDA in April 1999.

Action Plan Policy for 22,000 New Jobs in Wales
19 April 1999

1. Action by WDA

WDA cost in Wales £8.1m

WDA annual jobs budget £200m

Take half of the jobs budget and:-

Provide £5,000 per annum for three years, (renewable subject to funds) per employee, taken on by business in Wales.

Conditions:

Employees taken on full time on at least a minimum wage.

There are 58,000 small businesses in Wales, therefore with a 50% take up, there would be little unemployment in Wales.

2. Outcome

Little unemployment. No let off for dole cheats. Less boredom and crime. Culture change to get up in the morning.

3. Obstacles

(i) "The Single Biggest Obstacle to Business in Wales are Welsh Councils" "Old Labour" retired, male and totally alien to the small businessman.

(ii) Change in Planning Policies

Planning decisions are decided on the merits of the individual and not the applications. Decisions are ultimately at appeal, political and subjective. There is no faith in the Ombudsman by small business. The Ombudsman is unaccountable and un-representative of business matters. The Welsh Office have been paralysed by the abuses of the planning system (by all sides) and have failed small business.

(iii) Environmental Excess

The over protected Heron and Hawks are eating and killing all the newts and songbirds respectively, but the farmers and developers will be blamed.

There has to be a better balance between business and the environment. Currently it is all stacked against business. No one speaks up for business for fear of the Environmental Lobby. Small businesses do not have the resource to fight against such a well organised group.

(iv) Votes –v- Jobs

The politician in a local community gets 100% more votes to stay in power, from the unemployed, pensioners and others. They take a risk helping small business people against jealousy and the need to turn the Country into a Rural Museum. This is a challenge to the Assembly for which I do not see a solution.

4. Being Positive

There are thousands of Developers, Entrepreneurs and Business people who can help Wales if they are given the incentive and confidence.

The current Government policy on business, is, I quote:

> "Work hard with business to create
> jobs and a strong economy"

Can the political parties back a real policy such as mine, or are we to put our trust in Gossamer Promises?

Give the small business in Wales the financial support to turn round the Economy of Wales and we <u>will</u> deliver.

Many attempts were made to follow up this proposal. The best the WDA could do was to send the following, unsigned, critique. No-one, it seemed, could back this rebuttal.

T he saddest thing was that all of the new AM Leaders of the time, Alan Michael, Rod Richards, Mike German and Dafydd Wigley all received copies. None can see the negative past and possible future. They have blind faith in the WDA.

Can anyone remember Rhodri Morgan's views on Quango's, especially the WDA?

And, finally direct money for jobs as part of the New Deal is now actually in place, directly instigated by Gordon Brown, Chancellor of the Exchequer.

(B) WDA "Thoughts" Critique

RE: Action Plan Policy for 22,000 New Jobs for Wales

Employment subsidies of varying sorts have been used historically as a means of managing the displacement of workers in declining industries and attempting to create growth in an economy. However there are a number of problems associated with such proposals.

- Such employment subsidies involve huge opportunity costs (i.e. by allocating money in such a way, it could reduce resources which may go to firms which would provide greater employment growth overall – the 'gazelles' or faster-growth firms).

- They could also have little impact on the long-term competitiveness of companies. For example, the success of firms not only depends on the number of people employed but also their overall competitiveness; marketing, production, exporting, selling etc. Typically scarce resources of development agencies are used in this way, known as supply side improvement, rather than to artificially create employment i.e. it looks at improving the competitive position of firms first so they can grow and employ more people rather than the other way around.

- Furthermore, the number of people a firm employs depends largely on the level of demand for the final products and services that it helps to produce. Therefore any employment gains resulting from the subsidies are likely to be short-lived, unless the demand for a firm's products and services is increased in order to help pay for the increased wages of the extra employee, e.g. if a firm employs one more person without any increase in demand then costs go up and profit is reduced. Employing one more person increases the potential supply of the firm (i.e. what it can produce) but it does not directly affect the demand for what the person produces.

- Increasing demand in the longer-term is therefore the key to allowing more people to be employed. With longer-term changes to the structure and characteristics of Welsh firms (e.g. moving into new sectors and products, and becoming more productive then) such proposals are likely to be short-term in their nature and fail to achieve their objectives.

Economics department
July 1999

Welsh firms have expertise, but . . .
Where is the help?

Sir, – Local business can generate wealth in the Swansea, Neath and Port Talbot area. That is, local, indigenous, "been here for years" Welsh business people.

Inward investors have reasons of their own for coming to Wales, exporting their profits and leaving when they want.

Like the London taxi driver said: "We have taken the money off the Arabs, we are currently taking the money off the Japanese, who is next?"

Where is the help for the Welsh small businessman? I am sure if you were to give the £17,000 per job grants given to the inward, usually foreign, investors to the local businessman, he could take on one person or buy new plant to generate work for another.

The problem lies at the pointed end of the government in Wales. The big businesses have to deal with the WDA, professionals who can commandeer green field sites (and there are usually empty factories down the road not suitable), provide rent and rate-free periods and most generous grants (ask Lancashire) and all this in weeks – deals, planning, cash.

Meanwhile at the other end of the scale, the small businessman has to deal with the council or Tec consisting usually of "ex-some other council job, moved to keep in employment" person with no funds, no experience of business and no incentive other than to keep his job.

This, combined with the need for expansion or development, leads the beleaguered businessman to the council, usually the planning department, and local members.

It is my opinion that the majority of council members revile small businessmen and their ideas; add this to the council's own resident Nimbi's and it leads to long and procrastinated planning applications, refusals and appeals.

Neath Council turns everything down on the grounds of visual intrusion.

While foreign companies move to green field sites in what seems like weeks, the indigenous Welsh businessman is bogged down for years with no financial help at the end.

You may ask yourself why businessmen have not spoken up before, but the problem is that the small businessman is rushing around trying to stay afloat, complaining to the Ombudsman for local government, joining the Federation of Small Businessmen or the Chamber of Trade. Unfortunately these so-called safeguards have their own cosy relationships with local government, creating even longer, demoralising delays.

Please believe me, I am not in favour of raping the country at any cost for jobs, but local business must be helped. I have tried writing to my MP and the Prime Minister to invite them to listen to local developers, entrepreneurs and businessmen (Debs), as they promised in opposition, but they arrange photo sessions with happy businessmen while we all know things are not well.

They fear that to look at the council's approach to small businesses would open an enormous can of worms.

In writing this I have been negative and will be attacked, but you do not have to be Labour or speak Welsh to be Welsh, non-political and loyal to your country.

I ask this new government to meet the Debs in open forum to start to solve the problems of unemployment and poverty in South West Wales.

Debs (Developers, Entrepreneurs and Businessmen)

The Times, 5 January 2004

Labour plans to build on countryside

- Need for jobs outweighs Nimby concerns, says rural affairs minister

By Valerie Elliott Countryside Editor

John Prescott plans to strip local councils of their power to block building on green field sites as part of a policy to create more rural jobs.

He will target the Nimby (not in my backyard) mentality of shire councils who can halt any development by designating an area worthy of conservation. He wants to reduce the grounds on which they can reject new building.

The plan to create industrial jobs and the conversion of agricultural buildings into new homes was denounced last night by rural campaigners as "a pox on the countryside".

Critics fear that Mr Prescott's vision for rural Britain will simply create unsightly new buildings and conversions as villages are allowed to spread into the green belt.

Ministers hope that the move will bring more jobs and prosperity to some of the most rural areas.

For the first time, building projects will be given the go-ahead in the remotest rural villages, which have been strictly protected in planning laws.

Projects most likely to be approved will be those encouraging tourism and renewable energy, such as wind farms and biofuel refineries. Local authorities will be unable to reject developments "for the sake of the countryside" but instead must consider specific tests such as impact on character or beauty or the diversity of landscape or wildlife.

The plan for change is being finalised by Mr Prescott's Office of the Deputy Prime Minister. Ministers believe that it signals that the Government is intent on securing a future for rural areas, especially after reform of the Common Agriculture Policy.

The right for councils to designate local places with a special conservation status, such as the Aylesbury Vale, is to be scrapped. In future, green field development may also be allowed if there are "wider benefits" from farm diversification.

Planning controls will also encourage people who wish to develop horse riding, breeding or livery facilities and new homes for people who need to protect farm animals or crops.

Barn conversions may be allowed to create homes for low-income or key workers; otherwise, there will be tighter controls on "standalone" homes.

The final vision is expected to be announced at Labour's rural affairs conference in Manchester this spring but ministers have already sent out draft guidance for consultation. Ministers have been swayed by complaints from rural entrepreneurs, farmers and land owners about negative planning decisions which stifle new business ventures and prevent job creation.

The Countryside Agency, the Government's leading adviser on rural matters, broadly supports the need for change. But the Campaign to Protect Rural England said that the planning bonanza will bring "a pox on the countryside".

Tom Oliver, head of rural policy, said: "The Government has made the fundamental mistake of failing to value the ordinary, everyday countryside for its own sake. The landscape between our rural towns and villages, its beauty, tranquillity, biodiversity and heritage, appears to be regarded as a blank sheet of paper on the developer's drawing board."

Alun Michael, the Rural Affairs Minister, defended the planning shake-up. He told The Times: "We don't want rural Britain to become a museum of the landscape. Planning rules must make rural communities fit for the 21st century. Otherwise we could just make it impossible for people to do business in our rural villages and that would be tragic. There is a need to diversify the rural economy because the numbers of jobs in farming and land-related business are just not there any more."

David Curry, the Shadow Secretary of State for Local and Devolved Government, said: "If these reports are true, it would appear the Government is planning to ride rough-shod over the feelings of local people."

The Greatest Con in English History

I was eating chips when John Smith died
Not my party, but a man of mine.
In business we have no time
Other than to mark the paper,
Not my party, I cried, but a good man.

Kinnock had the vision of the green cross code
With unilateral Foot far behind,
He stood his ground on reds and those in town
But sandy beaches, and his land
Conspired to lose when he had won.

The Old were un-electable
Suicide notes and no middle policies to show,
Only faithful donkey tailors,
Tory haters (some their own)
Were waiting for New Government.

So a New one was spun
With a big smile and the right words
Ministers prudent, new jackets and ties,
And the right policies and the right words,
The timing was right.

And four years on
Am I the only one who will shout
"But are these his clothes"?
To a nation that has been duped
By the Conservative Leader – Mr. Tony Blair!

14.02.01

Devolution

What is the agenda –
For a man to vote himself out of a job
The best job in Wales?

What is the Agenda –
For a party to make itself weaker
To take a direction that splits the rails?

It's Devolution. Parting, partition, separation,
I don't like the sound of Devolution.

But, the Labour Party won the election, they had the mandate from the
    people for Devolution!
I did not vote Labour. I could no longer vote Conservative, and I am not
    Liberal.
I put the country before party and voted Referendum, but that is now behind
    me.
The people who did vote Labour did not necessarily vote for Devolution,
    they voted to get rid of the Tories.

Scotland will be Devolved, Wales will not! Davies will resign, eventually,
slowly, to save face. Michael will provide future stability. So why take this
route?

What is the Agenda?
For a party that can provide so much for so many
To take such a risk.

What is the Agenda?
That will allow the Taffia to rule
Have promises been made
To the Men Who Rule Wales?

Written on 10th September 1998 with a copy for Vincent Kane (BBC) 'Meet for Lunch',
Trinity College Carmarthen, Wednesday evening 16 September 1998.

Abstention

April 2003

The Talking Shop needs votes this May
To bolster their cred, sustain their pay
Policy flows for all to please
Promises made, forgotten with ease.

But another group control in Wales
Old Labour Councils rule the waves
Slimy Russell, Creepy Crawley,
Glamorgan (Gazette) Jones
The Welsh Ashambly just pick the bones.

Old LABOUR, Old Labour, oh how they fear
Power being lost, no sandwiches and beer,
To a brick built proportional way
Down Pussycat Bay.

Old Labour Councillors, pensioners, male
Business haters, oh how they fail
To see how development
Could revalue Wales.

Why do our politicians find it so hard
To support their traders, fill in the card
With a yes, go on, work and employ
Instead there is pique, refusal is the ploy.

Back near the hole, at the capital spend
Rhodri quacks, like all one legged hens
While Mike keeps checking on how much he earns
New Socialist Plaid, blames Bourne & Cairns.

While all this festers, voters yawn
And another factor begins to dawn
Could it possibly be? Sanity? Hope?
That no one will vote.
<u>For any of them!!</u>

This poem was written by a non-Welsh speaking, non-ethnic, disenfranchised majority vote Welshman

Adolescent Wales

The Ugly Town Poet, proffered as the culture of Wales
Lived like a Lush in the alleys midst the ales.
His lifestyle was no role model to awe and admire
Though his observations showed the hardship, depression and mire.

These desperate views of poverty and despair
Are replaced in this century by a much different care
By celeb names with just a thread of Wales
To fill the newsreels the post and the mails.

Catherine's in the Marriott, Charlotte's run off (again)
But Sir Hopkins deserted, such a shame
But this land of myth and legend, and editors tense
Can hype any story west of Offa's fence.

Back to our Dylan, next the anchor on the quay
Both holding Wales down with singular twee
Like our politicians and names established and bland,
Who fail to find vision in this wonderful land.

But let's not break this drunken fixation of past desperate souls
Or start looking for invention this side of the tolls
Which will make us all proud, not resentful of win
To speak our minds must remain a sin.

To debate and push forward radical thinking
For all parts of Wales, to Leave the Capital blinking
Is not what is wanted in the east or the west
To stay as we are is thought the best.

The majority of people vote for their own
For male pensioners who, with their families grown
Think only in their circle, where their footsteps sound
Have no interest in others, for life in the round.

For the people of Wales do not really want change, or
Betterment, quality, economy across the range
To drink and to fume like the hero of the bay
Will remain the benchmark for the rest of our days.

What do you think?

15.08.03

Conservative Hope

The Conservative Party has forgotten its roots
With strong support for directors and 'Boots'
Without direct help to followers in pain
Loyalty to the party will be on the wane

New Labour (old Labour in Wales) sets to look after its own
Staunch help for its voters has seen it grow
Poverty and poor are Labour land
The Conservative Party must take their hand

To show them that the people should hold their wage
Spend it their way in the Millennium Age
Not on social boxes, filling the towns
Ghettos of voters, strange as it sounds

Years it will take, to get the voters back
Individual helping will get them on track
Direct help and help that expands
Will bring the big prize back to Conservative hands

27.10.03

The Dictatorial Benefactor

Vision is not a thing to be found in Wales
Not in our leaders, the W.A.G.'s with their tales,
The approving of bus passes and sitting in the right rows
Is a very long way from making Wales grow.

A Dictatorial Benefactor, a leader, a mayor,
Would make the decisions to make us stare
At belief in ourselves to create Project Vision,
Not allowed by committee decision.

Infighting, backbiting, pique, the party line
Would disappear with calculated risk in time,
The wasted days on seating arrangements
Could be focused on the constructive engagements.

That would provide for Wales the following log
Of project vision known and bogged
By bureaucrats cowering in fear of mistake.
Let's elect a Leader, we've decisions to make.

Like a North South-rail, give it a whirl
The Severn Lake, the biggest in the world,
With waste disposal and leisure joined
Add water power, and the project is coined.

Close the Pembrokeshire smell, develop the haven
To make Winchester wince, invite the world, be brazen,
The projects reel off, one after one
A Dictatorial Benefactor would have apathy on the run.

27.10.03

This poem originated from a chance conversation with Welsh Office Planning Inspector, Mr. Wilkes, who suggested the reasons why Wales is the third world nation it is.

Why Do We Spite Our Own?

In Italy and Ireland, in France and Spain
Their people's fend their own, not give them pain
Helping their neighbours, easing their mind
Making life better for all of their kind.

Why in our country is hurt meted out
By bureaucrats, councils, officers with clout?
When a Yes makes life easier , no harm in this Yes
But the power says No, you're put to the test.

What must be remembered is this 'No' continues employment
For the power behind this negative deployment
Fills the bureaucrap files, costs out of audit
The applicant and enforcer, fail to sort it.

But it does get sorted at the end of the day
The applicant eventually gets their way
But the pain and the money that this 'No' has cost
Would have benefited All. Instead it's been lost.

So let's start a culture which helps our own
Yes, if you can. Yes, do go on.
Everyone happier, wealthier, no mess
If it is wrong, a No. But otherwise, Yes.

05.11.03

42

The News in Wales

Opening the pages, gives sweetness and light
Edited stories with deadlines tight,
Custom in printing, stories which warm
Good News Wales, loyalties torn.

Wales news spin, legend and myth
Utopia Ashambly, never a tiff?
Avoiding this reporting would dry up the print
Against Local Authorities who warn with a hint

That to show in the headlines "too" much hate
Will hold back local stories, closing the gate
Giving a propaganda slant to all of the news
Restricting the wounded from giving their views.

Business success, awards for all
Booming economy it must not stall
W.D.A. Quango's – ex bank managers – more spin
Are reported by Mary, forever a win.

Reality is different, money is wasted
On service consultants, grants are not tasted
By the wealth makers few
Recycled investment? Fairness would be new.

But Objective One will save the day
Economic problems will all go away

-You have to be joking –

The power in Wales that controls the press
Is the Local Authorities holding their cards to their chest
Trumping Ashambly with their powerless talk
Keeping editors neutered, scoopers can walk

So what do we do to rescue our news
Ordinary people must be allowed their views
Unedited letters, pages not ones
Give honesty to readers and a future for our sons.

05.12.03

Rabble Rouser

How many are there, in our streets and towns?
Do their numbers exceed us? What are the bounds? Are we the minority? Has
the count been done? Should we retreat, or be on the run?

Is it a class thing, or poverty or wealth?
Is it ingrained or taught? Creeps up with stealth?
To make the end user differ the most
The growing cancer, honour now a ghost.

Antisocial behaviour, road rage, graffiti
Smokers are litterers, fill hospital beds, burn their settees. Is the trigger that
crosses the border
Attention seeking deficit disorder?

These are today's rabble, to be feared with dread
And their numbers are growing; old values are dead.
Cool Britannia, makes sick on Spain's waves
They are the 'in' crowd, the rest of us slaves.

The Tories backed basics, our Tony agrees
The Liberal Democrats are waiting to see,
But our country must tackle this rabble today
Failure to do so will give Britain away.

Our Politicians should lead us, an example be known. The rabble debated,
community values shown. Brave leaders must guide us, with no shake of the
hand. To retain Great Britain as a pleasant land.

The Richards Report

Lord Richards has a job before him
But are those questioned singing the same hymn?
Should all those questioned give up their time
When Europe leaders have written the rhyme?

Ashambly powers greater or small
Are being debated behind Offa's wall
But what has been missed in this view of Wales
Is this interesting story, the strangest of tales.

Clapham Ron, in his need to win
And get a Yes vote, did a grave deed, a sin.
He persuaded the Councils in return for support
To be immune from enforcement, in the streets, or the Court

An agreement to rule Wales in the shop of the talk
The Ashambly, The Dove, The Councils, The Hawks
Lord Richards can question for the rest of his days
It's the Goodways' and Joneses that rule our Wales.

But overall control will fall without hustle
To the unelected masters in Brussels,
Wales is to be positioned in a region of nine
Lord Richards' report a waste of time.

17.12.03

"Suspended Skate Egg"
Second best by Ron.

Turbines White

Revolving wings, turn in the night
Feathered lollipops painted white
They sit on the hills, gathering wind
Thoughts of camouflage mysteriously binned.

As if to say, 'Here I am!
Planning Permission, catch me if you can!'
The majority want these powers green
But why on our earth do they have to be seen?

Paint soldiers' colours to hide these earners
Landscape power sources and fossil burners
For wind offshore, 'sky-blue tint' and 'bits of sea'
And get congratulations for energy free.

18.12.03

Lottery Justice

Money buys justice, let's set that away,
The Legal Aid poor, they're OK.
It's the majority of people that the system fails,
Lottery justice in England and Wales.

The lawyers and QCs cost the earth,
Modest claims are not the worth,
But when desperate fairness is needed or sought.
Only by re-mortgage or debt can justice be bought.

While over the fence the celebs and sports,
Break all the rules, the fouls and the torts,
Then bring in the system to defend their wrongs,
Time waste appeals, barristers with gongs.

The majority look on in desperate disbelief,
Looking for thousands to get their relief
They risk all their money on riskier laws,
On riskier lawyers with bottom line paws.

Take care on this path of lawful redress
Think hard: is it worth it to remedy mess?
Only use the money that helps to defend
There is no natural justice for the majority in the end.

29.12.03

Radio Ga Ga

Crass is a word that comes to mind
For the opinionated DJ's of the radio kind
With switched on giggles from their brainless hens,
Spouting witless comments from their disco dens.

This is a small poem, for small minded men
Whose end is in sight, dismissal in the lens
For when the audience counters come into place,
Our button press changeover will expose their disgrace.

For we are in charge of their contract bind,
These ballerina show offs, critical and unkind,
Their opinions and hurt can be cut at a stroke
Choose music, not prats. Give the listeners the joke.

02.01.04

50

Timeless Teams and Groundless Force

Does Baldrick think that we are really fooled,
By his three day dig, information pooled
Ooh-arr leaping in foundation deep
Only minutes to dig, no time to sleep.

Archaeologists tell me that you must not rush
That painstaking hours with trowel and brush
In an area the size of a workman's hand
Would be needed to excavate a finger band.

Television 'takes', the 'links' and sound
Would mean no time for digging could be found.
So come on Tony, let history know
How much time is spent on your show?

And Charlie and Tommy are not far behind
In fooling the public; instant gardens, are we blind?
We can't see your workmen, the 'real' boys.
Another of television's brain-dead ploys?

And finally we await the property slump
Makeovers, escapes and refurbishes to dump
Oh! hang on there a moment, let's just see
With them losing their money – I might agree!!

04.01.04

51

The Murder Box

The Murder Box which sucks our existence,
Assumes naivety and brain resistance
One hundred murder choices per week.
Cabot Cove's not a place to seek.

Midsummer death on a scale so grand,
Average community population slump, this land
Tooled up slaughter, our children to see
American death afternoons, Agatha for tea.

And the television folk with their bloodstained brains
Consider this carnage will cause little pains,
To our young people watching from unguarded boxes
While unsuspecting guardians spend more time on foxes.

It's in the home where lie our fears,
For our children and their brainwashed peers
See no harm in brutality, beating, blood and death,
Casual torture, removing of breath.

So you must not wonder why, in this age of our day
That bullying antisocial actions and murder in play
Is perceived as normal by multi-channel men,
But is something the rest of us condemn.

The blame lies clearly in this murderer's face,
But the box has the power, the position, the place
To deny and cajole then take their pay,
And live in the hope the problem will go away!

06.01.04

Dragon's Eye

Why is it that a Welsh Political Programme, which unlike
The Welsh press, cuts to the quick of Welsh Politics,
Exposes truth and humbug and rejects party propaganda
is scheduled by the BBC to miss its target audience?

It is obvious that in discussion with David Williams
He enjoys the feast before him. I would suggest
(please BBC) one hour, Sunday 10.0 a.m. – 11.0 a.m.
The W.A.G's and Wales need the Scrutiny.

07.01.04

The next referendum in Wales
(will be delayed)

More power is needed at the barrage build
The hole is filled and there's now formed a guild
Of National Socialists (Plaid) and loose cannon Reds
Who seek grandeur office, and to get into bed.

But Lord Hain can see from a much bigger scales
That a referendum is required by the people of Wales
To increase the wages the office and say
Of the W.A.G.'s "Tax raisers" at Cardiff Bay.

This voting action holds a much greater fear
For the devolution Maestros but no one will hear
They're blind to the dangers in the questions on card
For the voters on seeing will find it hard.

Not to vote them 'Out' and curtail their powers,
To take revenge on the 'Yes' vote in those wee small hours
So cunningly contrived by Peter and Ron
The Leader of the House and the Caerphilly Don.

So the W.A.G.'s will stay AM's to chat on all day
Discussing seating, construction and increases in pay
And at the cabinet office in the House of Real Clout
They will smile, Westminster Rules – W.A.G.'s all out.

11.01.2004

Jimmy's Dream

U-turn Tony has cast the die
But what is the question I hear you sigh
Will the vote we have be clear and cut
For it will be categorically, democratically,
Unanimously NO, but!!

They'll have another vote, they'll change the words
Lord Hain and Michael are first reserves
To fudge the issue, was it hunting ID cards
Sorry, Europe, keep issues simple, thinking hard.

No room for democracy, majority of men
(Women and children)
Percentage of voters, we need a win
Lies, damn lies and statistics, we need a win
Make them vote again, we need a win
(We know best)

Our referendum Jimmy, can now rest easy
We supported his journey, his vision, his war
He saw un-elected quangos from business were sleazy
Money in pockets, rotten to the core.

But the message to voters is to think on your feet
As this question to vote disturbs your sleep
With autonomous regions and us all in the boat
In Europe at arm's length must be your vote.
"Bet on it Jimmy"

If a fudge is put forward, vote no
Clearly, decisively, no risk, vote no
Never run off a miss hit, no lifetime pain
No stress, no danger, no loss of face,
Start again
"You can Bet on it Jimmy"

* Jimmy is Sir James Goldsmith

55

Banking on Success

If we could drag them out to man our phones
For a month and a day to look at our bones,
No flesh to see in this business world
Just Bureaucrap, delay and criticism hurled.

Bank Managers sit in their offices, conditioned
Courses on loans and debt, repayment permission
These Plc's make profits so grand
But on whose back does this work burden land?

No manager would return to his warm office floor
After suffering face-on at the small business door
His conscience would fail, his sympathies stored
No hard-nosed refresher to leave businessmen gored.

But cannot the four high street (sharks) fish
See that to listen, and help, and succumb to the wish
That the blip in the finances for the man in the shop
Can, dealt with properly, make everyone's profit hop.

But what do we get with our present four?
Telephone banking, ring one, two, three and then some more
Your banker is on long-term sick. Ring next week.
We'll relieve you of some money if you need to speak.

You telephone a.m. but the operator's harassed.
Is it Cynthia in Wick or Habinda in Madras?
"It's oursourcing cost-cutting in countries afar."
It's actually unfriendly, delaying and a mar.

And all the while that overdraft permission
Has cost you stress, delays, stoppage and indecision
You would like that manager to make your day.
There has to be another way.

14.02.2003

Bureaucrap

Bureaucrap (used liberally in this book) is
A word to describe the New Millennium
strain of bureaucracy. This hybrid strain
was first reported in 1997, is now almost
out of control.
Bureaucrap directly supports public sector jobs
And therefore public sector jobs vigorously promote
Bureaucrap.
Bureaucrap has however, a major weakness
In that should the private sector decide
That it is no longer cost effective to
Continue, business will close its doors.
The writer expects this shut down to commence
From 2007.

08.01.04

Puzzle Pages

Puzzle One

Circle the <u>correct</u> statement:

(a) Lord Hain has always sat on the fence.
(b) The first politician to be parachuted into Wales was Lord Hain.
(c) Lord Hain lost his principles, post Arms Park.
(d) Lord Hain is our greatest example of a Career Politician.

If your answer resembles an Audi Grill Badge, you have got it!

Puzzle Two

(a) Does Russell Goodway O.W.E. (Order of the Welsh Empire) even care?
(b) Does Edwina Hart cause a draft?

Puzzle Three

What do Paul Murphy, Lord Hain, Lord Hunt (Con.) and Alan Michael have in common?

Answer

They would, (if required) confirm that their Leaders can Walk on Water.

Puzzle Four

Can 'Old' Labour MPs be prosecuted under the Trades Description Act?

Someone Said It

John Prescott is the rivet that holds New Labour to Old,
There will be the most almighty crash
When he falls out!

I am not sure whether "Middle Earth" was in
Lord of the Rings or Harry Potter,
But I think that Rhodri Morgan came from there.

I think Mike German was neutered by Jeff Jones,
Propaganda Editor of the Glamorgan Gazette.

Is Nick Bourne an Ethnic Minority?

Paying students to stay in school
Would be subsidising jobs
And the jobless (SEE WDA critique)

Do North Wales MP's find the heat oppressive
When they come to Cardiff?

Lord Tebbit (The Chingford Strangler)
Should get to meet David Davies (The Monmouth Cosh)

Plaid Cymru "The Party of Wales"
Are as Cohesive a Party as the voters of Wales.

The Welsh Economy (1)
The Risk Takers and Wealth Makers
(And When they are Gone)

The Taxation System works Thus

Every day 10 men go for dinner, total bill £100. They decide to pay their bill the way we pay our taxes, i.e.

The first four men (the poorest) pay nothing

The fifth man paid	£1
The sixth man	£3
The seventh man	£7
The eighth man	£12
The ninth man	£18
The tenth man	£59 (The Wealth Maker)

All ten men were happy.
The restaurant owner was happy, he rounded the bill to £80
The group still wanted to pay their bill the tax way.

The first four men were unaffected, they would still eat for free

They realised that £20 divided by 6 is £3.33, but if they subtracted that from everybody's share, man 5 and man 6 would be "paid to eat"

The restaurateur suggested reducing each mans bill by roughly the same percentage.

The fifth man (like the four) paid nothing

The sixth man paid	£2	(instead of £3)	(3 pc save)
The seventh man	£5	(instead of £7)	(28 pc save)
The eighth man	£9	(instead of £12)	(25 pc save)
The ninth man	£15	(instead of £18)	(22 pc save)
The tenth man	£49	(instead of £59)	(16 pc save)

The first four men still eat for free.
The other six were better off.
Outside the restaurant, the men began to compare their savings.

"Out of the £20 savings 1 only got a £1" said the sixth man. "He saved £10" pointing to the tenth man.

"That's right says the fifth man, "I only saved £1, he got ten times more than me"

"That's right" said the seventh man, "why should he get £10 back when I only got £2" <u>The Wealthy get All the Breaks!</u>

"Wait a minute yelled the first four, we didn't get anything at all. The system exploits the poor!!"

The nine men were suffering strongly from the Welsh Disease (Resentment of Success), surrounded the tenth man and beat him up.

The next night, only the first nine men turned up for dinner, sat down and ate their meals. When they came to pay the bill, they found that they did not have enough money between them to pay, not even for half of it.

This is how the tax system works. The people who pay the most get the greatest saving on a tax reduction. If you tax them <u>too</u> much for being wealthy, they may not show up for Lunch.

My Government Policy Wish List
Manifesto 2005

Law and Order

1. Split the Police Force into two separate autonomous categories, crime and traffic
2. Privatise criminal catching
3. Three serious criminal strikes – life imprisonment (remember Tony Blair!)
4. Legalise all drugs – take the profit out. Remember American alcohol prohibition?
5. End the costly nanny state – No ID cards, more real freedom
6. Replace speed cameras with "your m.p.h. boards" Get traffic police back on our roads to sort the real bad motorists, private and commercial

Home Office

7. Strong low cap on immigration, schools to provide Sir James Goldsmith's "The Trap" as required reading
8. In Europe, but not governed by Europe. Our politicians are being led and brainwashed toward an unelected club. The differences in the Country's members will cause jealousy and rift.
9. Truth in Government, or you are out ten years, maximum. No career politicians.

Protect (but control) the House of Lords (the second house). It is our only safeguard against bad Government.

Abolish all two tier Government, make it Local Government or Regional Assembly's. This Country cannot afford, or want, both.

Business

10. Review foreign investment – end arm sales abroad (they are killing us with guns we made?) No jobs or business outsourcing.
11. Bann all food imports that do not meet UK Food Agency Standards

Insurance Companies

They are running amuck. Pension funds, accident policies – your house for your life......

These people are becoming the leeches of our Society who released these awful people on us.

Domestic

Litter, graffiti, chewing gum, damage to the community assets.

We need draconian laws to rid us of these Acts.

Planning

The planning system is strangling the Country. The Government will take years to sort it. In the meantime, ban directly subjective decisions.

Quack – and then they were gone

On a Thursday in June, Welsh voters rose
And laid low the headlines of my little prose
The day Labour's leaders fell like leaves
Their powers to voter thieves

Who robbed the voice of the Goodway clan?
Gone is Jones, and Crowley ran (with the cash)
But who will replace these powerful men,
Who now conspire in smoke filled dens?

It's an interesting time for politics in Wales.
Could dinosaur Labour sink 'neath the waves?
Proportional reps rule with leadership qualities?
Out with a century of dinosaur loyalties!

My money is on disarray, bicker and biting,
Spinning for power and salary writing.
Oh, how we long for leadership and vision,
To work hard for Wales and an executive decision.

26.06.04

Quack, quack, quango gone

The Welsh Ashambly's Labour lead
Quango's gone, it's Rhodri's deed
Says Dragon's David, he's always said
He'd kill them off. Well, now they're dead.

Hawker gone, first Water now Business,
Quoting civil servants as brain dead and listless
The writer's opinion thinks the Bay life would suit him
With or without them, small business looks grim.

But hang on a minute, there's the Chancellor's speech?
Civil servants in thousands with lost jobs will screech
But set this aside, there's a principle at stake,
It's Gordon that's decided on the Quango fate.

To balance his budget, Mr Brown has decided
To occupy the pay time of AM's derided
As unoccupied, lacking in venture and workload
You'll do the job in-house, our Rhodri has been told.

Is this the autonomous WAG men so few voted in
London instructed to downsize and employment to bin
But the question Welsh business will ask with fear
No money last month, no money next year.

But Welsh small business could not get any money anyway!

16.07.04

My friend

My friend called John, he's Jack
I met him forever, and back.
His left leg is straight, has a boxer's hand
An electrical trade with mortar and sand.

He rode on a bike in a foreign fight
But an accident dislodged him with terrible spite
Many visits to theatres, medicine and pills,
Failed to divert him from his business and bills.

Lights needed fitting in pubs and hospital – mental
Patients in corners, endangering the rentals
His business sound, a lifetime success
Semi-retired as college store man no less

We argued and threatened when we met at first
Had it gone any further I would have hit the dirt
But somehow or other a friendship bloomed
An easy time for work mates clearly doomed?

His energies still, at his extended ages
Are inventing, prototyping, investigating pages
He makes me laugh, a peak to cry
He'll be my friend 'til the day I die.

Holiday No 7 – Loire Valley

Why two bridges to cross a river?
We asked ourselves
Our first view after sent a shiver
The double island made us well

Giselle was kind, a smile, efficient, welcome France
Read our meter, showed the bikes,
She left us happy, we did a dance
Home for a week, two little tykes!

No telly, vacuum, what would we do?
We drank the freebie, Domaine de St. Mar
Grapes and crackers, 12%? Where's the loo?
It's revolving upstairs, don't drive the car

We're planning big things, read the comments
Tanks and zoos could do the trick
Missing the telly causes some lament
Prepare seven day schedule, God we're slick

What's in the shed? It's locked out there
No keys we've got will lay it bare
Storing wood? Have they got a dog?
A peek inside – I espy a cog (It's a well!)

I'll finish here, we're allowed a page
Giselle may check, there'll be a fee
We've been here five hours, it seems like an age
Six and a half days to go, I need a p… another glass

Written in the visitors book, Gite No. 7
07.04.04

Solicitors – (The Reality)

Loyalty and Trust, Professional code
Big brass plate, dress formal mode
Emanate efficiency, end of their nose
Hard crust paper, fast on their toes.

The reality creeps up, dare you speak
Did they say that? Your nerve ends creak
Sign up last month, or was it more
Dare you check, fear to implore.

These professional people, they must know best
They are up to speed, put your mind at rest
But the time goes on-and-on-and-on
You pluck up courage, something wrong

It's not with us, we wait in line!
But it's in your out tray, awaiting sign
Poorly paid clerks, tired of grind
Pay the big-brass plate, little mind

Your customer cred', then takes a fall
How dare you question such a person so tall
You duck for shelter, you have so much to lose
And the system continues……

Saturday night fever

(also inc. Sun, Mon, Tues…)

The ratings have dived, no one's there
The telly producers, they don't care
Reality TV, American crap, channel pits
Lie in your chair, eyes glazed, no wits

But there's hope out there if you care to look
Walk in the park, or read a book
But get away from the hypnotic screen
A year and a day to get your mind clean

Then start to think how to plan your day
Community, charity , football, play
Join a club, song or dance
Give limbs and brains and socialising a chance

And start to think that the telly spin
Decided for you, your information win
The bombs and death and bad news choice
Hides good news, majority and honest voice

So I've given the lead to trouble and strife
                        (and the kids, and you)
To use your time and get a life
Push the button down hard a signal to send
The End

The Severn Lake c2030

Placid and tamed, yachts stepping their masts
A man-made asset, income to the last
Business and development will follow the shores
Pride for the decision, contempt for the bores

Turbines and wave power align this dam
They started producing when the first concrete ran
The land-fill core-rams move a metre a week
Providing centre space sealed in, no leak

Lavernock meets Devon, employment for life
Paid for by tide and wave, waste cost site
As the years pass by the park top will flourish
Fishing and cycling on top of the rubbish!

Yachting and boating in a man made haven
Host the Olympics, twenty-thirty-seven
A target for Ashambly, something real to make
Let's do it, let's build it, the Severn Lake.

27.10.2004

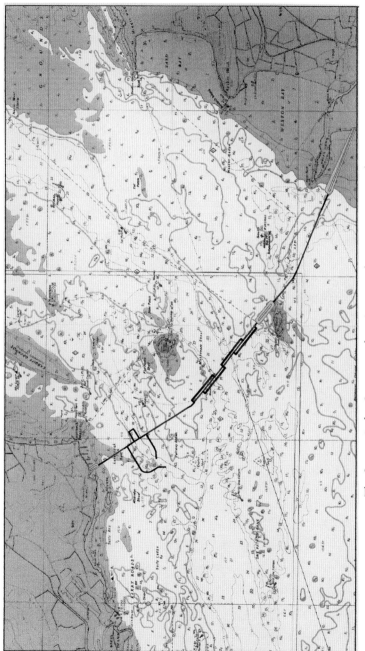

The Severn Lake Causeway that Creates 145,000 Hectare Lake

Motorway madness

Three lane motorways, Wales has two!
Majority of drivers belong in the zoo
Animals, reptiles, some species unknown,
Drive on our roads, molluscs their clone.

Middle Lane Drivers hog a road of their own
The rest of us 'go hang', small lorries just groan
Undertakers* cause danger, overtakers train**
To no avail these mindless MLD's have no brain

HGV's enjoy an evil of their own
59mph is their maximum zone
But the motorway police will never them book
Try 55 at Port Talbot and you're on their hook

Cameras on poles, in vans, stuck on bridges,
Big Brother is collecting, the cash grows in ridges
Wales is being fleeced of speed and cash
From the booths on the Severn to the cop at Mountain Ash

Two lane carriages, hill comes into view
Overtaking lorries, stuck like glue
Mile after mile cars build up and scream
Phone 0800 "good driver" not on our team?

But here is a way for government save
Don't upset the motorist from cradle to grave
Motorways cost millions, more road, we want plenty
Look on the left. The slow lane is empty.

04.09.04

* Motorists who pass on the inside lane, not mortuary attendants
** Pass the MLD clods and settle in lane one, smugly

Help for small businesses

A. HELP

Do you want help to start a small business, but you are looking for a product, manufacturer or sale base, or just any business just to be a self-employed one-man-band?

Contact our web site – but no promises.

Location

Do you want to know which counties in Wales to bring this business to?

Do you want to know which counties to avoid?

Do you want sound finance, to know which banks to avoid and which banks are fair? (in the strictest confidence?)

Grants

Do not waste any time and certainly no money in chasing grants. The WDA was set up to pay consultants and ex-bank managers high salaries and to contribute to expensive glossy (and God, have they been glossy) magazines to expound the virtue of the chosen ones. This does not mean you. As the WDA no longer exists, any money will now dissipate within the Ashambly.

B. INVENTION AND INNOVATION

Do not under any circumstances:

   a) part with any money
   b) tell anyone your idea
   c) agree to a joint venture with anyone

Regarding an invention, lock the idea in a cupboard. It will be stolen. You will be robbed and that is worse when you have parted with money as well.

The cost of safeguarding an invention safeguards jobs at the Patent Office and those of your very expensive Patent Agent.

The Idea will still be stolen

If it is not stolen, you will fail to keep up the payments.

One good idea can cost you a minimum of £25k over 8-10 years. The vultures will be waiting!

Do not join inventors' clubs. It is a highly paid lecture circuit for those who have succeeded.

One day they, (and for that matter, the government) will all listen to inventors and instigate a proper system of patent, which will safeguard invention and its production in the UK. That is a long way off. Remember, lock that cupboard.

Good advice
Finally, remember what you read in Bureaucrap on page 40. My advice is to go and spend three or four years cleaning boats in warm marinas in Southern France. There will be plenty of businesses going cheap after 2007.

C. CONSULTANTS – SOLICITORS – DEBT COLLECTORS
(the grasping society)

All of the above start charging, (at today's prices) from around £130 per hour, plus £1,000 per day. Yes, One Thousand Pounds per day. This is because they work from the best offices in town. More than half your bill is just to pay their own rent and rates.

Business Consultants
Provide a report on all the information you have provided to tell you what you already knew. They take no risks and will not guarantee their advice. Most are ex-bank managers attached to Government Agencies. Just think about how many bank managers you know that have gone on to run their own businesses.

Solicitors
1. Make mistakes and charge you for it
2. Always disagree with the other party – it's a good earner!
3. Since deregulation have evolved with the "blame and claim" culture to be the pits of our society.

Debt Collectors

If you receive a demand from the new breed of debt collectors, beware. They buy debt and they will hound you for their chunk. They are ruthless, uncaring, and the new danger to small businesses.

Big companies are renowned bad payers. Small companies will, as we approach 2007, find cashflow problems. The big companies with a double whammy, sell debt. The vultures, usually London based, have legal and insolvency departments and also in house bailiffs. They will bankrupt you in 21 days.

28.8.04

Short Fat Slimy & Fundamentally Corrupt
(The Book to Follow)

Our Rod did meet these awful men
Not every day, but now and again
Council leaders, male, sixty five
Arrogant, obtuse, barely alive.

Few voters voted, but they got in
Voting for your own, is not a sin
But these union ex's, miners voice
Business haters, give no choice.

Low cost houses, stay on the "sick"
You are well looked after, we'll wield our stick
Votes at Westminster to fatten the cash
100 year socialists, no need to dash.

But one council leader, down by the sea
Bust pool old Rod, and we'll agree
Rod's 'slimy' outburst plus deeds in town
Stacked one by one to bring him down.

Mindful of progress the other machine
Deselected males for varnish and preen
But back in the valleys, the conveyors still out
Rod Richard haters. Who still have the clout.

16.10.2011

The whistle blowers

The whistle blower knows that the wrong has been done
But these colleagues are friends, when they know they will shun
Close ranks, cover up, keep the deed out of sight
Knowing it's wrong, saying it's right

A terrible dilemma for the servant that's good
This wrong will hurt others, uncover you should
But look at past blowers, the harm they become
It is they that become evil, not the deed that was done

Loyalty to the Company, the Council, the Firm
Comes before honesty, the truth to confirm
Loyalty to our friend to hide the misdeed
Cover up culture the way to proceed

But what of the owner of the error or hurt
This cover-up culture then starts to revert
It is they who are then guilty of accusing the wrong
How dare anyone question, such an honest throng

While all the while the audit tills gleam
Time spent checking, complaints procedure, team,
But the checkers themselves start hiding the truth
One of our team is wrong? That would be uncouth

So the wrong drags on endless, then a principle glows
Then the wrongdoers fall out, nervousness grows
Long term retirements zoom into view
The wrong is put right, ranks close like glue

And then the whistle blower is the target for venom and spite
With the wrong righted, and owner out of sight
Demote, transfer, ostracise, sack
No wonder this culture stays firmly on track.

05.09.04

77

Is Wales a nation?

Lloyd George, when asked on a visit to Aberystwyth, was Wales a nation, replied:

> "A nation is a land whose citizens, in their overwhelming majority, share a common culture, sense of identity, heritage and traditional roots."

I cry at our anthem. I'm proud to be Welsh and live in Wales. I do not speak Welsh. I despair at the cost of the Welsh language to those who do not require it.

I fear those who would want to make us an independent nation.

Free Press for Wales

Can't anyone produce an honest, serious newspaper
Not tied to advertisers?
With investigative journalists providing
Both sides of a story free from Government
Or local authority cronies
Who threaten truth or input?

A newspaper open to any contributor with no censure
(other than legal or defamatory)

The satisfaction I have had from having a platform
In this book to inform other like-minded people of my
Thoughts, has been overwhelming.
Others must have a similar and free opportunity.

FREE WALES PRESS

The Great Welsh Milk Mystery

(Where has the 18p gone?)

I've milked a cow, not a difficult task
My mentor milked hundreds, shot straight in a flask
This accurate man filled bucket after pail
If he was milking today he'd take to the ale.

For it's the supermarket bosses who now milk the cows
Milk customers and farmers and have NFU* rows
Decide prices and quotas and who'll buy from who
It's desktop farming; don't know where it grew.

Now farmers are revolting – nothing new there!
Costing the country and tearing out their hair,
For they know what their cost is and what they are paid
They've sieved through the figures with pencil and spade.

They know the sales price on counter, in cup
Worked out the middle man and his mark up
But try as they might from toast until tea
They can't seem to find the missing 18p.

Supermarkets cry, "it's not down to us!
It's only 18p; why all the fuss?"
The farmers then cry, "well, give us the money
Our margins are low – we're not being funny."

And all the while the customers look
And place more black marks in the their little red book
And will slowly decide to seek other offers
Wary of the power of supermarket coffers.

06.09.04

*National Farmers Union

The Deep Dark Forest

Trees are growing wherever you look
Make furniture – stoke fires – paper for books
Except the trees that you see will be there forever
Protected by orders in book bound by leather.

They are gathering in numbers, covering our land
Lost open spaces that were once grand
Darkness is descending, arches of leaves
They're stealing our light these wooden thieves.

N.I.M.B.Y.* protesters use trees as their tools
To stop honest developments from roads to new schools
But the tree numbers now are starting to blight
Sympathetic removal will give us some sight.

The patchwork quilt that has made this great picture
Must recover its position, trees only in vista
Permission to plant would reverse the dark
Hedges and woods, yes, but keep more fields for the lark.

06.09.04

*Not In My Back Yard

The Secret of Success

(but don't let me put you off)

Hard work has been done by every
It helps but will never the win
You look and you know they're wealthy
Short time, no effort! A sin!

You can have the brains of Einstein
The capital tucked in the bank
It means diddly squat to the bottom line
And honours are not worth a thank

A silver spoon could start you
Old money to help you along
But if that secret ingredient is not due
None of it's worth a song

Big company – big training – barn storming
You would think would bring them through
Directors' breakfast each morning
Cannot stop the audit's red hue

So just settle yourself to your workload
Be more happy in work, not less
Wait for that turning, the right road
Signed – luck and timing – the secret of success.

02.10.05

Civil disobedience

Breaking the law is starting to grow
Minor infringements, current media levels low
But our Mr Blair on an appeasement to banks
Has set a course for swelling the ranks.

Law breaking first started with taxation high
Pensioners imprisoned, increased council tax – why?
Insuring cars, third party the min.
At first sight could not be considered a sin –

– But without insurance and cover, the licence came next
Binned log books came after, kept the DVLA vexed
Slowly and surely we are entering crime
It's easier each offence, easier each time.

Employers are also finding insurance far reached
Employee liability, laws are being breached
But what can they do, the Government care little
The parliament statute is starting to get brittle

And now on this day Welsh Michael has said
You'll be breaking the law hunting fox 'til it's dead
While 'Gordon the Tax' sets sights on tax and fifty
All middle England (and Wales) start to look shifty.

Law breaking scales unheard of or counted
Judges and Lords, handcuffed, dismounted
Mr Blair will go down, with his back bench leaving
As the Great British leader of civil disobedience.

08.09.04

The Parasite Economy

Parasites live off the life of the donor
With economy, money and the business owner
The parasite thrives and loves a loner
Attacks all his systems like an abattoir boner

Whilst the entrepreneur produces and sells
The army of parasites expands and swells
The current economy our information tells
Provide business -v- parasites, ringing huge alarm bells.

The parasites are in order of merit
All government department, Councils take top credit
Lawyers who claim, That Entourage, That Debit,
Health and Safety, Insurance Companies – Euro Law – and there I end it.

For the list grows on by the day
But let us look back, not lose our way
For the verse three group are making hay
Expanding, promoting, subjective the power, increasing their pay.

But what if the donor dies?

3.09.04

The Magic Roundabout

On the A48 at the Ewenny turn
Leaving Bridgend, our motorist must learn
That some psychotic planner of matters, roads
Has reduced all traffic to mindset toad.

Tryffids stalk, winking the red
Local vehicles stopped, better back in bed
Kerbstones protrude marking a course
But bad language frustration makes drivers hoarse.

For their journey will be blocked by a system benign
For the next light rule will stop the line
And the hope you must have is to be, 'next the light
For if you are three cars back you are in for a fright

For the pretty green light which has signalled your rivals
Provides traffic behind you which you and survival
Creates gridlock, queues, frustration and fog
Men (and women) and machines in a clog.

The most amazing part of our junction magic
Is that it continues in place of years of tragic
The newspapers local carry tattle most regular
Yet the road block continues for ever and ever

Will the council or traffic management
Consider or scrap, roundabout return, tryffid banishment
"No, not until the idiot that thought it up takes early
retirement on health grounds."

8.09.04

George's Law

Blame culture corrupts, bankrupts, chokes
Business, employment, economics and growth
Employee falls over, cuts finger, blows nose
Employer pays insurance, covers heads and toes.

Lurks behind brass plaques, sinister suit
Lawyers, barristers, a system so cute
That plays poker with business, with their much bigger hand
Small business lays transfixed, how many grand?

Five for a finger, two for a toe
Employees must go
Insurance ineffective, is it worth the risk
Blind with the screen, cut finger on disc?

A contract must defend the small business man
Employees taking responsibility for the work of their hand
Offering an honest agreement to indemnify their employ
To work with the employer, to share in the joy.

Of income for both, not an industry of blame
What's good for the gander, the goose gains the same
So let's draw up an agreement, a contract to draw
Where responsibility for oneself is George's law.

09.09.04

A Grumpy Old Welshman's Wife

(written having consumed a large glass or three
of Cabernet D'Anjou. Dated 09.09.04-ish)

She's always there when you need her
She's always there when you don't
She washes pants, irons vests, pours the beer,
"I'm off for a bevy before tea love," – "Oh no you won't."

She's the sensible one of the partnership
You know that she's right when you're wrong
You discuss every move on life's long trip
Go it alone, remember, there'll be a hell of a dance and a song.

She watches you eyeing the other gender
Through eyes that seem elsewhere
Just remember your socks and their mender
Don't think she hasn't a care.

Medallion man has a chrome bike
A soft top, two seater and a blonde
What he really needs is a slow trike
And it's the third time he's forgotten his bond.

For him, life is not all that certain
The warmth and comfort, fraught
It's not so good, behind that curtain
With what half of the money has bought

The Grumpy Old Welshman is carried
With sensible clothes he is spoilt
He loves the woman he married
– And so he should!!! xxx

12.09.04

87

Litter (20 years on) Who Cares!

Up the agenda, more on our minds
Not afraid to say, with discussions abound
Those dropping litter penalised with fines
The country's fed up, is this the turn around?

Smokers are litterers, look in their cars
Fag ends on corners, empty the trays
But no longer their fug blocks out the bars
The country fed up, their changing their ways

Smokers cause fires, block hospital traction
But their mess on our streets, there's 90%
Leads us wanting attack. Zero tolerance action
To stop their littering, we must use out intent

Shout 'litter' aloud so that all can see
That object grounded care-less-who cares?
That the litter polluter is ousted and seen
The country fed up, the country cares!

18/09/08

Deep and Savage Cuts

Lord "Mr. Macorber" Hain predicts Welsh pain
Cuts to health, the public sector slain
Cuts, deep cuts, Tory cuts sub prime?
Too savage, too soon, the Labour Party line.

A liberal right, turned Labour left
Trotsky views written, have forests heft
His party leaders can walk on water
Is the line given and spun to order.

Tax and spend and spend lots more
Spend us out, banks open door
Has been three terms of Labour spin
Wait four years and let us win.

Mr. Macorber needs a voice with pre Lord
Promotes debt and jail, not cabinet award
Twenty shillings spent with nineteen earned
Live within means, not money burned.

Neath P.F.I. Hospital is his local debt
His party's career spokesman forever inept
First to invent expenses scam
Deputy Prime Minister, never this man!!!

Tax and spend is always their way
Dennis Healey with begging tray
Their worries, little. More public sector pay
For the Tory cuts will save the Day!

14.15.201

My Uncle Bert
(for Dianne)

My father had a Francis Barnett 150cc motor bike. It broke down, difficult to get parts, not much power. Then he bought an ex-army Royal Enfield 350cc.

Although very young, I took interest. Always there to see it start, there to feel that heat when it returned from work, or a trip to Canton, Cardiff laden with my mother and many bags. But there were other bikes. St. Brides Road saw Cement Works bikes, dusty, tired and big. Llandow Bikes, small, noisy, cheap to run, and, St Athan RAF Bikes, Sunbeam (green) Velocette (black) even 'bang bang' Harley Davidsons – these bikes gleamed from worn out polish dusters, were silent from excess of grease and oil, but all to a future mechanic, were 'toys for boys' .

Then, one day, as I came ambling along from school, around the corner of the Star Inn, I froze. In my sight, outside our house, not next door, or next or next, but our house, was a 'motorbike'. Chrome, more chrome, Blue in colour...... 'whose was it, why was it there'. I ran. I ran faster in case its owner started up and took flight. I arrive. It is chrome. Lots of it. Powder blue, black dual seats, foot pedals I wanted to put my feet on. Chrome headlamp with two chrome winkers. Side lights and, what is this sitting on the petrol tank, a chrome rack. For a bag! My sandwiches! A tool kit! – a chrome rack. Then, my eyes locked to the name – Triumph. Both sides, and down the side oil tank T120. I came around from 'dazed' to 'amazed' to wanting to touch.... But no, who does it belong to. Are they in my house. Who owns this lovely chrome toy.

From the back door came a familiar smell. Not cooking....(not Welshcakes) (not even washing).... Through the back kitchen to the living room... it was pipe smoke, Old Holborne. There sat 'My Uncle Bert'

I knew him of course, from going "up the house". My father's term for Garfield House, Pen-y-Mynydd, St. Brides. As a young boy growing up, I always thought "up the house" rather a challenge. The place was packed with lovely, warm women that seemed to 'like me a lot'. They always wanted to pick me up, give me a hug and cover me in kisses. Didn't seem to get much of that in the wrong playground in school (boys one end, girls the other).

My grandfather had died a year after I was born and there were only two men. Billy, who I did not like at all, and he did not like me, and another man who was always at work. This was my mother's brother Uncle Bert .

Today, this Uncle was in 'our' house and from the conversation I heard, had arrived by chrome! Things had changed. I gave a welcome smile, and a big hello (which surprised my mother I can tell you).

Uncle Bert , was, to me, a big man, braces, heavy brown corduroy trousers, strong boots and a check shirt. He had a big warm kind face and gave me a big smile. From that moment, we liked each other.

I hung on every word. My father also loved bikes and wanted to know the engine size, miles per gallon, how many pistons, top speed, how many gears, did it have a stand, were parts readily available? I just wanted to know if I could have a ride on the back!!!

The conversation went to work. I went out to the front of the house to have another look at the chrome. By now, a small group of lads from our road had gathered around the chrome – "is it your fathers' – no it's Uncle Bert's from St. Brides, he's taking me for a ride in a minute" !!

On cue, Uncle Bert came out of the front door, fitting a black helmet with a funny peak, onto his head, there were glass goggles on the peak, but as Uncle Bert wore glasses, they were little used.

We all watched. My father. My mother from an upstairs window. Half the village by now, and of course, me. Levers were moved, throttles were twisted, stands were removed and a small chrome rod covered in rubber swung out from the kick start. A heavy boot rose and rested on this peddle. If bets could have been taken, they would. Powerful leg, one kick, the Triumph T120 chrome burst into life, almost as much as my pride, a gear selected, high revs and the powder blue chrome Triumph T120 disappeared...... That was my Uncle Bert I boasted, good bikes, Triumphs. One kick, did you see? Donald Roberts from No. 13 turned for home. "I think he forgot to take you"!

The visits to Garfield took on a new edge, especially if we all went by bus. We would be dropped by bus at John David's corner, (Funeral Directors) in St. Brides, and would walk up to Garfield. I would always want to stay to see 'my' Uncle Bert...... more like to see 'that bike', my Aunty Ann would say. We would have large slices of bacon pig that would be brought from the pantry, hung up, dry cured, covered in muslin cloth, or home made faggots and peas. Then, when Uncle Bert had eaten his dinner, he would always offer to take us all 'down to the bus' A motor bike sandwich – three on a bike...... Heaven!

"Bert's sold the bike"! my mother informed me...... he has bought a van"! My heart sank. My chrome rack will never have the chance to hold my sandwiches. The T120, thirty pieces of silver for a van?

We visited Garfield on a Saturday, very rare, and there it stood. Around the back with geese lying comfortable in its shade. A Morris Minor 850cc van. Split windscreen, green twin doors 1952 year (in good condition). Everyone went inside except me. Uncle Bert came outside. I thought it might be a different check shirt, but he always looked the same. "What do you think"? I had, at that moment, no opinion...... "its for a bit more room" I said, thinking rather unkindly that my Aunty Ann took up too much room on the chrome. "Have a look at the engine" he lifted the round bonnet to reveal a gold painted engine and everything clean and in its place. "I'm going down the yard later, do you want to come"? "you bet"...... Permissions were sought, advice given to Uncle Bert about keeping an eye on a wayward boy, strong warnings to me about behaving myself and doing what I was told (never have been able to grasp that one...) This was, as far as I know, the first time anyone was to look after me, freedom at last.

By the time we got to Ricketts' Farm Machinery (David Browns a speciality) at St. Brides, turned left (or right) at the Pool Mill pond, I had forgotten all I knew about bikes. Vans were in. Vans were transport!!!

At that time, Uncle Bert was driving the lorry for Dai Ricketts, delivering and collecting farm machinery throughout the Vale. But a new venture had, that morning, just started. Farmers were buying ever larger tractors – more power, more pulling. What farmers now needed were bigger trailers. None were readily available. This, of course, I found out from Uncle Bert many years later. What I also learned was that, ironically, the man that arrived, in what was in those days, a very expensive Land Rover was Glyn Thomas from Monknash. It is very likely the trailer that he bought that morning, along with another two later, were being towed by me whilst 'on the hay' in my school holidays, ten years later.

Uncle Bert had a rare skill that he shared with his brother Ted. He could weld. Ted was taught by the B.S.C. Uncle Bert , just picked it up. His unique skill was – "he could weld 'upside down'" that is not to say he was dangled from a rope. He could weld from below the object being welded and still have a total strong bond.

Dai Ricketts would buy up wheels, old lorry bodies, steel tow pins etc. Uncle Bert would put it altogether.

On that Saturday morning, I stayed in the van. I didn't mind that. I wobbled the gearstick, pressed the button on the handbrake – "do not touch those keys" invitingly dangling on the dash. Opened the glove box, loads of goodies in there!

On the yard, there was much hand shaking and back slapping, crawling on the floor, kicking of tyres, writing on notepads. The Land Rover left. I thought Uncle Bert would shake Mr. Ricketts' arm off, but he (Mr. Ricketts) seemed to enjoy it. Uncle Bert came to the van – "you all right"? "why are the keys on the floor"? "I'll be back in a minute". I watched in fascination as Uncle Bert backed the lorry up to the trailer and was amazed to see a wire pull the trailer neatly on board. "Ready for Monday" he said. Those were the only words spoken until we got home. He never said a word about the keys, he didn't need to!

That night the Morris Minor Van took our family all the way to Wick. Boy, did I long to visit Garfield (and Uncle Bert) after that. The track from Garfield to the main road was all grass. The Morris Minor Van's tyres dug into the grass causing ruts. Old stone, ashes from the fire – all were put in the holes and ruts. (On visiting Garfield 2010, there is no grass – there is now a tarmac road – 'from small beginnings')

Boys play football, spend time on farms, chase girls and eventually run wild or away. Family visits grew less, to none. My Uncle Bert married my Aunty Ann, had a daughter Dianne, needed and bought a bigger van. I had a motor bike for my birthday, Broke down. Hard to get parts. No power (heard that one before!!) Took it for trials to Garfield. 'hard to think now that Dianne used to sit on a towel on my petrol tank and scream – "go faster" '

Years went by and I was reaching the end of my apprenticeship with advice from my Senior College Lecturer at Bridgend to "get into heavy machinery – get experience from a big plant and machinery" All I wanted was to get out of the garage I was working in! "Your Uncle Bert is coming to see you tonight" was all that I was told. I had not seen him properly for years. He still liked green vans. The one he now had blocked out the sun on our house.

My mother, who had 'gone off' Old Holborne told me to show Uncle Bert the garden. He sat on a barrow full of dry grass cuttings, smoking his pipe, tapping it out, refilling, puffing away – I had visions of the grass cuttings catching light. I don't think he would have moved!

He explained all there was needed to know about obtaining a Green Union Card. "You had to have your apprenticeship papers, A National Craftsman Certificate etc. etc. meet at Llantwit Town Hall at some ungodly hour, swear at somebody "and your in"

To be frank, I was mystified – "why was I to go to all this trouble" I asked. "Because I have got you a job at Aberthaw Power Station" he said, "is that big enough for you"? Well, you could have knocked me over with a T120. "I'll see you Friday night. Wear some proper clothes". Now, I loved my Uncle Bert, but I was not going to wear braces......!

Friday night came and went. I walked up the steps of Llantwit Town Hall with Uncle Bert, sat in a dimly lit room for an hour listening to union officials expounding the merits of membership. Was given a neatly folded green membership card, and found myself in the car park, leaning on the 'Green Goddess' quicker than you could say 'closed shop'

Uncle Bert explained that the Power Station would only accept fitters that held a green card, and said he would look out for me last week of August, Monday morning, prompt!

Wally Green was a slight, neat, important, down-to-earth man. He did not like his 'white engineers overalls' but he had obviously earned them. "So, your Bert's nephew" "heard a lot about you". I tried, but I just could not at that moment, see my Uncle Bert extolling my virtues. However, "he's not here this week, gone to a tractor rally down Cornwall"

Wally took me on a tour of the power station garage, brand new. "Moved up from the prairies down there, we're all on staff status now." "It's a new world." "Got all we have wanted for years." "They have realised how important we are."

My first thoughts were that I had arrived at the right time. Later on that year I went to the 'prairie' garage which confirmed it.

"Your Uncle Bert built this, what do you think?" I looked at a huge contraption with bearings and shafts, big plates with holes and what looked like a ships steering wheel. I was very 'unimpressed' At this point a forklift in the far side of the workshop drove across to where we were, Uncle Bert's mate, Ron Collins, had been steam cleaning the most enormous dumper engine you had ever seen and brought it to this huge monstrosity. With Wally guiding, me looking useful and about six bolts! The engine was attached to a mechanical mystery...... You could, now, stand on rubber matting, turn the wheel and completely strip down the engine, put bolts and parts in bins for refitting etc. etc. I was very 'impressed'....... "That was my Uncle Bert"

There were five groups of fitters at Aberthaw. The day shift, (Uncle Bert etc) and four other shifts – A.B.C. and D. I worked on A shift. We only met day fitters one day in five, so it was not surprising that it took about three weeks before I actually met up with Uncle Bert.

I was in the main hall machine shop waiting for a part to be welded, I had been on since 6.0 a.m. and it was about 8.10 a.m. The welder, a sort of relative, had been talking about Bert. "Just watch" he said "here he comes." Across the main walkway strode Uncle Bert (I think he had on another check shirt!). Newspaper under arm 'into the toilet' "He's a man of regular habit, he'll be out at 8.30 – on the dot" and, he was!

I only worked in Aberthaw for two years and a bit. Good garage fitters were promoted to turbines and eventually I was. Uncle Bert wanted to stay in the garage, but there were no jobs in the whole of the station he did not know. We used to talk for hours in the garage, each time more than he had ever said before in the whole of the time I had known him at Garfield.

Men play football, spend time on farms. Get married and eventually get tamed. Families drift away with jobs and ambition.

I lost my Uncle Bert from afar, but when I look into Dianne's laughing eyes, he is there...... and, I think, he has a new check shirt......!

Gareth
15th August 2011

Georgie's

East of Pyle, M4, Junction 37
You will find a breakfast from Georgie's heaven
Men of work in white vans arrive
In droves, in hoards, like bees to a hive.

Our Hayley and girls, cook and deliver
At first in a hut that was only a sliver
But extensions go North and sun rooms went South
No advertising required, just word of mouth.

All matters run smoothly, efficient and calm
The milk and the bacon and eggs from the farm
A quiet man moves deftly through the busy bees
Everything perfect, the food and the teas.

Customers are known, no kedgeree required
Distance no object for that full plate desired
Meetings and plans are cued to arrive
The taste and the service are worth the drive.

So if you're in Wales and wanting a meal
Avoid motorway hills, lacking appeal
The A48 twixt Pyle and Bridgend
Turn on the roundabout and take a left bend
Arrive Georgie's

Lewas-ap-Foote

Wild and Windy Wick

The Beacons Rise looks East at Wick
First catches sun, but snow can stick
St David's spire a centre end
Community hamlet with help to lend.

'Thomas the News' gives famous days
To carnivals, cricket, YFC ways
The veggie show at village hall
Usurped, Y Felin by bat and ball.

'Best Kept' Doug did years and tries
But never quite could win that prize
A village sore took that win
Beat grass well cut, and litter binned.

The future's well for those to recall
James and Jones, Morgan and Small
A Jubilee event, like 'seventy seven'
Will send burning message from Wick to Heaven.

11.12.2011

The Beast

In the late 60's, my wife and I opened a mobile caravan on the top car park at Southerndown selling trays of teas & coffees, home made sandwiches, welsh cakes, hot dogs etc. We worked most of the summer weekends, sometimes until 11.0 p.m. at night and gave a service not previously on the site. The following year we were out-tendered by ice cream vans.

On Friday 29th July, we visited Ogmore-by-Sea, and at a tea van, bought coffee, tea and "the beast". The Beast was a plate sized bap, with bacon rashers, and more bacon rashers, and eggs, sausage, mushrooms and, and, and......
Unfortunately, at our age, there is only so much pleasure one can manage! It was, though, delicious.

Sadly, we learnt that this busy little business will face a similar doom to ours in the 60's.

We realise in these lean times, tender money is needed and rules are in place, but cannot the local authority's score the service and value to locals and tourists alike in their decision making, so that "the beast" can continue to survive an Ogmore downs.

G.G. & A.J. – 29th July 2011

Pembrokeshire, Land of Invention

In July 1999, I tried, along with a team from the WDA at Swansea / Cardiff, to sell an idea to Pembrokeshire Council that would make the County a magnate for UK business. I met Mr. Kevin Wakefield, Mr. Bryn Parry Jones and others. To the surprise of the WDA, but not to me, the idea was rejected.

The idea was that an Inventor with a new product has to find huge sums of money to protect his invention, let alone design, produce and market the product. Most small good ideas are stolen, and / or get produced abroad, usually China. The small Inventor, the entrepreneur will be devoured by the big boys – who have deep pockets to defend their wicked ways....... I personally have twenty or more ideas that stay locked in the cupboard.

The proposal to Pembrokeshire County was a legal deal to be struck with an individual Inventor to come to Pembrokeshire to design, make and sell your product from here and we, Pembrokeshire, will protect your invention (with an invention protection fund)

The secret of the idea was that no UK (or other) Company would steal products from the mouths of a County or Region.

Setting up such a proposal is relatively cheap, but the benefits and returns are huge. (Dyson in Gloucester)!!

Pembrokeshire, I await your call......

Pembrokeshire, Land of Saviour

The full details of all the work that was put into trying to get Pembrokeshire "Land of Invention" up and running in the early 2000's was also given to the Editor of The Western Telegraph on the 20th October 2011, with a promise that it would be published directly.

Perhaps the good people of Pembrokeshire should not bleat about jobs and investment arriving West, until they look more inward at their decision makers.

One envious decision to hide or kill an idea could cost thousands of jobs!!!

Lord Hain's Fence

Lord Hain reigns atop a long wide fence
China's wall would hold its length in defence
And the width of indecision and career protect
Leaves no-one in doubt to the reasoned effect

Many decades have steered the tanned man's course
Middle of the fence, guided information source
No dropping in roses, which could be ….
So stay on the fence with smiling grit

Strong socialist views were masked from Blair
Strong socialist constituency, local business despair
Many cabinet posts "a safe pair of hands"
From his wide fence platform he safely stands

Back comes the letter on conqueror flash
Telling of enquiries made, excuses attached
But if further enquiries are required
Do not hesitate to enquire c/o the fence

And the wide fence leads the Lord safely up
To ermine, the lifetime and the silver cup
A springbok route to an armchair seat
Stay on that fence, a career complete.

22.09.09
Calais Marina

Porn Day

Our little girl is six, her brother only eight
Their mother, our daughter
Greets them inside the school gate

The news has come by sender
She hoped would go away
The gay Blair babes agenda
School tomorrow, is porn day

The children given permission
For cartoons of this and that
May understand this vision
Now know why mummy is fat!

Why Harry loves Larry
And Elle's legs are wide
Though Timmy fails to grasp it
His soft bits wont go inside!

Next days revision, in the bike shed
And hidden on the field
Makes the pre teens confused, and brain dead
The porn day doom is sealed.

And the children denied the porn day
Not driven by time wasted wonder
Enjoy friendship and harmless child play
Oblivious to Government blunder.

The parents consider and remember
Education for their little mites
And chose schools without hidden agendas
Teach love when the time is right.
And at Home!!

And finally...

In this book you will have seen that I have been critical of local Councils and their alienation of business. Local party politics have, in the last one hundred years, kept Wales poor; this, a land of such huge potential with people and skills to match any.

I have also been critical of the Welsh Ashambly, in that it has no meaningful powers. The power in Wales lies with the local tribes, the 22 unitary authorities, some very good, some very, very bad – and worse, with no overseeing control. The people of Wales are starting to see this – even the Friends of the Earth in the mammoth link to the Ashambly website, recognise this.

If Wales is to grow up, the Ashambly must first renege on Ron Davies's promise to the Unitary Authority Councils and take full charge of Wales. Secondly, it must outlaw local party political vendettas, favouritism and the council culture of protecting mistakes at any cost. It would be important to eliminate the opportunity for a local council member to influence and in some cases, instruct the council officer who, it must be remembered, is a civil servant <u>and</u> his employee. The council member can promote or demote officers, leaving officers with conflicting loyalties.

Thirdly, the Welsh Ashambly must value and look after the indigenous Welsh small businessman. Stop money flowing to inward investors and then on to Korea, America, South Africa and so on. Stop the consultant culture.

And finally Wales must grant high value development permissions, not hampered by the Welsh disease, resentment of success. Entrepreneurs at the top, such as Sir Terry Mathews at the eastern gateway to Wales down to the lowly garage owner, struggling within Wales. They must be looked after for this alone will inspire others.

My prediction is that this will happen eventually, but after many years of denial (unless Wales comes up with a leader with vision – perhaps a dictatorial benefactor) ?

01.03.06